The Ac

a comedy
Peter Quilter

SERVING THEATRE

SINCE 1830

SAMUELFRENCH.COM
SAMUELFRENCH-LONDON.CO.UK

FOR PRODUCTION ENQUIRIES

UNITED KINGDOM AND WORLD
EXCLUDING NORTH AMERICA
plays@SamuelFrench-London.co.uk
020 7255 4302/01
UNITED STATES AND CANADA
info@SamuelFrench.com
1-866-598-8449

Each title is subject to availability from Samuel French, depending upon country of performance. Please be aware that *THE ACTRESS* may not be licensed by Samuel French in your territory. Professional and amateur producers should contact the nearest Samuel French office or licensing partner to verify availability.

MUSIC USE NOTE

IMPORTANT BILLING AND CREDIT REQUIREMENTS

Other titles by Peter Quilter that are published by Samuel French include: Curtain Up, Boyband, The Canterville Ghost, Glorious!, Just the Ticket, Duets, and The Nightingales.

CHARACTERS (5F/2M)

LYDIA MARTIN – THE ACTRESS (in her late 40s, 50s or 60s)
KATHERINE – HER DRESSER
CHARLES – HER ELDERLY FIANCE
HARRIET – HER AGENT
NICOLE – HER DAUGHTER (20s or early 30s)
PAUL – NICOLE'S FATHER
MARGARET – THE COMPANY MANAGER

TIME PERIOD IN WHICH THE PLAY IS SET

This fictional play is not fixed in a particular time period. So the play could be set in the modern day, or in the 1930's, 1950's, 1980´s, etc. It is up to the director and designer to decide on the time period for the play.

STAGE SETTING

"The Actress" takes place mostly in the star dressing room of a large theatre. The dressing table is covered with make up, souvenirs, tissues, creams, perfumes, cups, gifts and bottles of champagne. There is a record player or other type of music player (depending on the period chosen). The mirrors are all surrounded by cards from well wishers. The room includes a sofa and various chairs and is full to bursting with extravagant bouquets of flowers. There are framed and signed posters on the walls of productions in which Lydia Martin has starred at this same theatre.

The dressing room set takes up about two thirds of the stage. The other third is a second area representing the stage of the theatre where Lydia is performing. This area contains part of the theatrical set for a production of Chekhov's "The Cherry Orchard". It can be quite a bare set, just a vase, table, a chair, but it should evoke an atmospheric Russian feeling. In the upstage section of this part of the set, there should be footlights that point downstage. The idea is that the Chekhov scenes are played to an imagined audience that is upstage. So we watch the actors perform these scenes from behind them.

ACT ONE

Scene One

(Backstage at a grand theatre, preparing for the farewell performance of an actress named **LYDIA MARTIN**. **LYDIA***'s dressing room. Enter* **KATHERINE**, **LYDIA**'s *dresser accompanied by* **LYDIA**'s *daughter,* **NICOLE**. **KATHERINE** *immediately heads to the dressing table to tidy it up ready for* **LYDIA**'s *arrival.* **NICOLE** *stands in the doorway staring at the abundance of flowers)*

NICOLE. Has somebody just died…?

KATHERINE. They haven't stopped arriving all day. I can't clear them away yet. Not till she's seen them. You know how she loves flowers.

NICOLE. And how she hates flowers.

*(***KATHERINE** *looks at her questioningly)*

It depends entirely on who they're from. Don't you think?

KATHERINE. I wouldn't know. The last time anybody bought me flowers, it was – *(she thinks, no recollection at all of when it was)*… Oh…

NICOLE. That long, eh?

*(***KATHERINE** *clears some items from off of the chair at the dressing table, leaving it empty)*

KATHERINE. Here – have a seat.

NICOLE. I can't sit there. That's mother's chair.… No, she wouldn't like that.

KATHERINE. Then you'll have to clear the sofa.

NICOLE. I'd rather have a cigarette.

(She takes out a packet of cigarettes and puts one in her mouth)

KATHERINE. Nicole –

NICOLE. What?

KATHERINE. You know perfectly well.

NICOLE. I'll go outside, shall I? With all the other naughty girls?

KATHERINE. She has to protect her throat. Tonight of all nights. …Where will you be sitting?

NICOLE. *(Putting the cigarette in her mouth)* At the bar, probably. Call the stage door when she gets here. They'll come and find me.

*(**NICOLE** exits. **KATHERINE** decides to clear the sofa, putting various bouquets and bottles into gaps on the floor. After a moment, there is a knock on the door)*

KATHERINE. Yes?

*(The door opens and **MARGARET**, the company manager, looks in)*

MARGARET. Is she in?

KATHERINE. Not yet.

MARGARET. *(Looking around)* Gosh. Flowers.

KATHERINE. Yes.

MARGARET. She could open a shop!

*(**KATHERINE** forces a chuckle)*

…We'll go up late, the foyer is full of actors. It's deafening. Trying to stop them gossiping and getting into their seats could take hours. Even so, I thought she'd be here early. Speaking of actors - Michael says he's got a sore throat. "If he survives the show at all" he says, "by ten o'clock he's sure he'll have the flu". I told him – darling, it's the last ever performance, you can have *the black death* by ten o'clock and nobody will care. …Besides, the supporting cast are just set decoration tonight. All eyes will be on Lydia. Her grand exit... Are we missing anything?

KATHERINE. Just the wig.

(The phone rings, **KATHERINE** *answers it)*

Yes?... Not yet. *(She hangs up)*

MARGARET. ...Are you planning to steal something?

KATHERINE. What?

MARGARET. Her lipstick, her powder puff, anything? You really should stick something in your handbag. I've got my eye on a few little props. They might be worth something in twenty years. By which point none of us will be worth anything.

(She picks up and examines a couple of objects on the dressing table)

KATHERINE. ...Margaret, I need to get on with -

MARGARET. Yes, yes, of course... I'll track down the wig for you.

KATHERINE. Thank you. Have a good show.

MARGARET. I doubt that.

*(***MARGARET*** exits, closing the door behind her. A second later, the phone starts ringing again.* **MARGARET** *appears through the door)*

...Your phone's ringing.

KATHERINE. Yes, I –

*(***KATHERINE*** answers the phone)*

Hello? ...Right – thank you.

MARGARET. Is she?

KATHERINE. *(Putting the phone down)* She is.

MARGARET. *(Taking a deep breath before she speaks)* Hold on tight – it'll be a rough ride! ...Actually, I might call on her a little later. Let her settle in first. Hopefully all these flowers will put her in a good mood.

*(***KATHERINE*** is spraying the room with perfume)*

(Sniffing) ...Lavender?

KATHERINE. It helps her relax.

*(**MARGARET** laughs ironically and exits, leaving the door slightly open. **KATHERINE** now makes final preparations. She turns on the lights that surround the mirror, she opens the make up box, she pours a glass of water, puts the chair in its correct position. With this done, she stands away from the door and waits. A conversation is heard from the corridor. She sprays a little more perfume)*

LYDIA. *(Off)* I can't talk about it now, you'll have me in tears... Tell Michael it's only nerves – he should use some sore throat medicine. ...No, of course I don't have any.

*(Enter **LYDIA**, seeing the flowers)*

...Oh no! These flowers can't all be for me. No!

KATHERINE. Yes.

LYDIA. So many!

KATHERINE. People just wanting to say goodbye.

LYDIA. Don't make me cry. Too many goodbye's tonight.

KATHERINE. Margaret called in. No message. And Nicole is having a cigarette.

LYDIA. She came?

KATHERINE. She wouldn't miss it for the world.

LYDIA. Oh, yes, she would. Nicole doesn't like seeing me in a spotlight. She never did. It's very strange. Most people see fame as a gift, not an irritation. But she always did have an unusual view of the world.... Such flowers...

*(**LYDIA** removes her coat, which **KATHERINE** hangs up. She sits at her dressing table and looks at herself in the mirror)*

...Oh, my dear Lord...!

(She checks the bags under her eyes, tightens her skin)

...All these thousands of nights staring at this decaying face before every performance. At least I won't have to do that again. I'm having all the mirrors in the new house painted over. It's not a pleasant thing, watching yourself age in such detail. Every new crease and streak of grey. We cover it up with such skill. But we know it's there. By God we do. *(Excited by a sudden idea)* ...Shall we smash the mirror tonight?

*(**KATHERINE** is shocked)*

Why not? Throw a chair at it! Crash it to the floor in tiny, nasty pieces. Then they'll know I mean it.

(She slams her hand flat onto the mirror obscuring the reflection of her face)

Gone! Wiped out!

KATHERINE. ...Perhaps you need a herbal tea...?

LYDIA. No - brandy. I need brandy.

*(**KATHERINE** quickly locates a bottle of brandy and pours a glass)*

...Pour one for yourself.

KATHERINE. I just did. I'm pouring yours next.

(Chuckling, she pours a second glass of brandy)

LYDIA. We'll make a toast. But when we're done, hide it. Otherwise every character that comes in the door will want a glass. And I may need the whole damn bottle tonight.

(They make a toast)

LYDIA. To Katherine, for looking after me.

KATHERINE. Thank you. And to you – for such a memorable experience. I will never forget it.

LYDIA. Oh, that's - ...That's very touching. Thank you. I don't know why I'm so surprised.

I suppose we actresses think that all our dressers absolutely *hate* us behind our backs.

KATHERINE. Oh, we do!

LYDIA. *(Laughing)* But you'll miss me when I'm gone.

KATHERINE. I will. Everybody will.

LYDIA. Perhaps… But only for a year or two. Then they'll find some other home for their devotion. I don't mind. Keeping that candle burning is exhausting. Anyway – *(raising her glass)* …to Katherine.

KATHERINE. No. To Lydia Martin. Her grand farewell. A triumphant final performance.

LYDIA. Triumphant? I'm just hoping we get through it alive. Down in one.

(They drink the brandy in one gulp. They look at each other, smiling)

KATHERINE. …I'll fetch your wig.

(LYDIA nods and KATHERINE exits. LYDIA then wanders the room looking at all of her flowers. She picks up the phone and calls the stage door)

LYDIA. …Is my daughter outside? …Well, tell her to come up – I want to see her! - And tell her she shouldn't smoke.

(She puts the phone down. A knock on the door)

…Yes?

MARGARET. *(Off)* It's Margaret.

LYDIA. Not now, Margaret. Nicole is on her way up.

(MARGARET opens the door and pops her head in)

MARGARET. Alright - I'll give it ten minutes. Nervous? Excited?

LYDIA. Yes. *(Scowling at her)* Plus irritated.

MARGARET. I'll see the others first. The director has asked me to give you a few little notes.

(LYDIA laughs out loud at this. MARGARET is unfooted by that reaction)

…Perhaps I'll suggest he just writes them down and slips them under the door? I'll go and check the, erm…

(**MARGARET** *decides it is best to just leave. She exits.* **LYDIA** *examines some of the cards attached to the flowers and smiles. Then she finds another of which she disapproves. Her smile drops. She locates a pair of scissors and a litter bin and proceeds to cut the heads off of the flowers in this bouquet one by one.* **NICOLE** *enters*)

NICOLE. What are you - ?

LYDIA. They're from your father.

(**NICOLE** *reacts with a wry smile*)

NICOLE. I suppose it's better than flushing them down the toilet.

LYDIA. Yes, that would be a waste.

NICOLE. Can you stop doing that now?

LYDIA. No – I'm enjoying it.

NICOLE. Mum.

(**LYDIA** *snips off the final flower*)

LYDIA. Now you can give me a hug.

NICOLE. Now I can't be bothered.

(**LYDIA** *opens her arms to her*)

LYDIA. Nicole!

NICOLE. Too late. The moment's gone. It's all about timing – I would have thought you'd know a bit about that.

(*She sits on the sofa*)

LYDIA. No! You can't be mean to me tonight. I'm retiring.

NICOLE. Until you get bored in Switzerland. Can I smoke?

LYDIA. I will not be bored in Switzerland. It's beautiful, romantic, - clean. …And no you can't. I thought you gave up?

NICOLE. We don't give up our addictions in this family.

LYDIA. I am.

NICOLE. That remains to be seen – doesn't it?

LYDIA. Not at all. I'm in love, Nicole. Charles will give me such a rich, full life. I won't look back. I'll rest! It's what I always dreamed of. What would you have me do, die here in my dressing room after a million shows – alone, tired.

NICOLE. Better than dying cold and full of chocolate.

LYDIA. What?

NICOLE. Switzerland, mother. They have chocolate there. And snow. Didn't they tell you?

LYDIA. You're being unpleasant.

NICOLE. I thought I was being factual.

LYDIA. Well, you can go and be factual and unpleasant in the foyer. There'll be fascinating people for you to talk to. It's full of famous actors.

NICOLE. Oh – actors. *(Sarcastically)* Hooray! …I shall need a drink.

LYDIA. You can have some brandy. *(She points to the bottle)* But just a drop. I'll be relying on it this evening.

NICOLE. You thinking of doing the show drunk?

*(**NICOLE** crosses to the brandy)*

LYDIA. I'm thinking of not doing the show at all. So getting drunk might be the only solution.

*(**NICOLE** pours two glasses of brandy)*

…Will you visit me? In Geneva?

NICOLE. Maybe. I don't know.

LYDIA. Why don't you know? Don't you like snow and chocolate?

NICOLE. It's just Charles…

LYDIA. What's so wrong with him?

NICOLE. Does it matter? I don't have to like him. He's your choice. You're the one that's jumping in to bed with him.

LYDIA. Why is it all about the bedroom with your generation? You're missing the point. There's more to our relationship than sex.

NICOLE. Oh, I certainly hope so. The man can hardly get up the stairs.

LYDIA. You're being nasty again. Why are you being nasty again? Honestly, I don't know where you get it from.

(NICOLE *hands her one of the glasses of brandy*)

NICOLE. Yes, you blooming well do. Good luck!

(*She drinks her brandy*)

LYDIA. Don't say that. "Good luck" is *bad* luck in the theatre – you have been told that before.

NICOLE. I forget.

LYDIA. Lots of manure. That's what you should wish me. "Merde" – and lots of it. And do you know why?

NICOLE. I don't remember. Or I don't care – one or the other.

LYDIA. The opera houses in Paris. The horse drawn carriages bringing the rich people to the theatre. The more carriages, the more horses, the more people in the audience, and therefore the more manure on the road at the end of the evening. So that's why you wish the actors lots of manure. "Merde!"

NICOLE. And I'm sure tonight it will stink for miles.

LYDIA. Thank you, Nicole. What a sweet thing to say.

(**LYDIA** *now drinks her brandy.* **NICOLE** *looks closely at her*)

NICOLE. Are you alright? You look a little, erm – pale.

LYDIA. I haven't finished my make-up yet, that's all.

NICOLE. Is it?

LYDIA. …I'm feeling a little fragile. Perhaps I should just have gone quietly, with no announcement. Slipped away when nobody was looking.

NICOLE. Oh, come on, mother. And miss one more moment in the spotlight?

LYDIA. Yes, but tonight it might turn around and bite me.

(*Enter* **KATHERINE** *with* **LYDIA***'s wig mounted on a mannequin wig stand*)

NICOLE. Too late now anyway. Katherine's brought your head in.

KATHERINE. (*To* **LYDIA**) Charles is on his way up.

NICOLE. (*Pulling a face*) Oh, really?

LYDIA. He'll soon be your step father. So you be nice to him.

NICOLE. He won't be my step father – he'll be your husband. *I* decide who my father is, not some marriage certificate.

Enter **CHARLES**, *an elder and clearly wealthy gentleman, slow and unsteady on his feet. But with a twinkle in his eye*

LYDIA. Darling.

(*An embrace between them*)

…Look – Nicole's here.

CHARLES. Nicole.

NICOLE. Charles. (*A pause*) (*to Charles*) …Well, it's been lovely chatting with you. I'm going to the foyer. It's full of actors and I can't wait to get down there and hear all about – well, hear all about *them*. So you two do whatever you need to and I'll see you later…

(**NICOLE** *exits*)

CHARLES. She doesn't like me.

LYDIA. Of course she likes you! She just takes her time warming to people. She even ignored me until she was seventeen. (*Adjusting Charles' tie and collar*) You look very smart.

CHARLES. I came straight from the bank.

LYDIA. Everything ready for Geneva?

CHARLES. Oh yes. I'll soon have my leading lady all to myself.

LYDIA. Not long to wait. Just one final show. – Have you seen all the flowers?

CHARLES. I have. Are they all from handsome ex lovers?

LYDIA. Yes, they are, mostly.

CHARLES. *(Slightly horrified)* Oh. I was actually making a joke.

LYDIA. Were you? Ah - well, my darling, none of that matters now. You won the prize.

CHARLES. Yes. *(Looking at all the bouquets)* I just hadn't realized there were so many in the race.

LYDIA. Sit down for a moment.

CHARLES. No – we have guests, I have to be downstairs. I just wanted to wish you a wonderful night. And give you this.

(He presents her with a little jewellery box.)

LYDIA. Oh, you're so –

(She opens the box and it chimes a little melody)

CHARLES. The lady in the shop said it was a theatre song.

LYDIA. It's beautiful. Thank you.

(She puts the music box on the table and takes hold of both of his hands)

…I shall look for you tonight. *(To* **KATHERINE***)* Where is he sitting?

KATHERINE. Dress Circle, stage right box.

LYDIA. I shall throw you a glance during my big speech in Act Two. You make sure you catch it.

CHARLES. I will. I won't take my eyes off you. …The whole town is yours tonight. And I am the luckiest man on earth. May I kiss you before I go?

LYDIA. If you absolutely must.

CHARLES. I must. Absolutely.

(He gives her a very loving kiss)

...I shall count the minutes until I see you again. You make me feel sixteen years old.

LYDIA. You *are* my sweet sixteen year old. ...Now hold on tight to the railing or you'll fall down the stairs.

CHARLES. Bon voyage!

(With a cheery wave, CHARLES exits)

KATHERINE. "Bon voyage"?

LYDIA. He's not a theatre person. That's one of the things I like most about him.

KATHERINE. When do the two of you actually leave?

LYDIA. Almost immediately. He has members of staff that have packed up everything at home. So we just get a few hours rest and then the flight is tomorrow morning.

(LYDIA sits at her dressing table, preparing her make up, etc)

...I didn't want to stay around, dwell on everything. A clean exit. Though I'm not sure what all the rush is. Charles does everything slowly – he walks slowly, eats slowly. But this – it's all terribly fast. Perhaps he doesn't want to give me chance to change my mind? It's odd. I mean, we have so much time. From tomorrow we'll have nothing but time...

KATHERINE. Do you want to get dressed?

LYDIA. No, no. I don't want the curtain to go up on time! We'll make them wait tonight. You have to build up a bit of expectation. I want to walk on stage just at the point when they're wondering if I'll turn up at all. *(She adjusts her hair)* ...It's part of the performance. Being an actress is not just saying your lines.

KATHERINE. Not when you're a star.

LYDIA. Well, the public gives you that crown - and they can snatch it away from you very easily. The trick is to bolt out the door before they get the chance.

KATHERINE. Is that what you're doing?

LYDIA. Perhaps. ...Or maybe it's just love? I have no idea. Us actors rarely know how we really feel. Or – for most of the time - who we really are. If we did – there'd be no need to pretend to be somebody else every night, would there? We're all just one step away from the madhouse. ...Has the wig been dressed?

KATHERINE. Yes, we just need to -

(At this moment, **PAUL** *enters.* **LYDIA***'s handsome ex husband)*

PAUL. I'm just saying hello. Whatever you do, don't tell me to "get out!"

LYDIA. *(Standing)* Get out!

PAUL. Lydia –

LYDIA. I said "Get out!" - I made it very clear I don't want to see you again.

PAUL. That's not very welcoming.

LYDIA. I mean it, Paul! You have no right to be here. For god's sake – it's just before a performance!

PAUL. Well, I would have been here a bit earlier, but I had to help some old guy get down the stairs.

LYDIA. What old – ? *(Unfooted for a moment as she realises this was Charles)* ...Just go, please. I have no desire to be in your company.

PAUL. Oh, shut up! You can stop being an actress now - you're retiring.

LYDIA. You don't get to tell me what to - ...Paul, I mean it - just go!

PAUL. I certainly will not. This is my last chance to see you, and I *will* see you whether you damn like it or not. And besides – I bought a ticket. Yes, paid for it. Out of my own hard earned cash. And you're expensive!

LYDIA. Too bloody right I am. And worth every penny. You're lucky you got in! So now you can spend two hours staring at me on the stage and there's no need to see me now.

PAUL. *(Turning to* **KATHERINE***)* Hello. Are you a friend of madam?

KATHERINE. No, I'm not, I'm her dresser. I mean – yes, I am, I'm her dresser.

PAUL. And you've survived? Congratulations. The streets are littered with Lydia's ex-dressers. She used to get through three a week. Throw a stone out the window and chances are you'll hit one of them.

LYDIA. Stop it, stop it. That's not even remotely true.

KATHERINE. I've found her very pleasant to work with.

PAUL. You're not serious?

KATHERINE. And you're not very nice.

PAUL. Oh, I'm delightful. You just have to warm to me.

LYDIA. Why don't you just leave us in peace and go down to the foyer? I am sure there are lots of people down there you can annoy.

PAUL. I'd much rather cause trouble in here.

LYDIA. You always were insufferable!

PAUL. Did you get my flowers? I sent lovely flowers. They must be in here somewhere.

LYDIA. *(Smiling broadly)* Oh, yes, the flowers. Yes, I did get them.

*(***LYDIA** *locates the stalks on the floor, from the flowers she beheaded earlier. She holds the stalks up proudly)*

…And they *are* lovely. So thoughtful of you. Find a vase for these, would you, Katherine. There must be a rank old jam jar at the stage door somewhere.

*(***KATHERINE** *takes them and edges to the door)*

KATHERINE. I'll see what I can find.

*(***KATHERINE** *exits)*

PAUL. Don't you get bored with all this theatricality?

LYDIA. No, I don't. But I get very bored with you. So it's not a feeling that's unfamiliar. How did you even get backstage? They're very strict. There are always dozens of young admirers trying to force their way in, but they rarely get to see me. Unless they're hopelessly good looking or disgustingly wealthy. And you don't qualify.

PAUL. Nicole passed me through.

LYDIA. She should know better.

PAUL. She knows more than you think. Though she hides it very well, I think our daughter is rather clever.

LYDIA. Yes, she gets that from me.

(LYDIA sits back at her dressing table and touches up her make-up)

PAUL. ...You look beautiful.

LYDIA. Oh for God's sake! I know that!

(PAUL crosses to the sofa)

PAUL. Whoever this chap is taking you off to Switzerland – I hope he realises.

LYDIA. Well, he's not *blind*, if that's what you mean.

(PAUL sits on the sofa)

PAUL. ...Is he here tonight?

LYDIA. That's no concern of yours. - Don't sit down! You've not been invited to sit down!

PAUL. Keep your voice down, Lydia, they can hear you in the balcony.

LYDIA. You need to go - I'm expecting friends.

PAUL. What friends?

LYDIA. Important friends, *nice* friends. All my ex lovers.

PAUL. *All* of them!? We'll have to move the furniture back.

LYDIA. *(Intrigued)* ...Jealousy, Paul? From you?

PAUL. No, no. I've sent you out into the world now. I know you get hungry and you can dine on whatever takes your fancy. We had our time together. And that's that. It's a memory. A souvenir. Though I still can't quite manage to shake off the feeling that it was enormous fun while it lasted.

LYDIA. Was it? It's so long ago, I can't say I remember.

PAUL. Ah but you do. And that's the problem.

LYDIA. There is no problem, believe me. I'm very relieved not to be married to you.

PAUL. But at least I *did* marry you. Nobody else has managed that.

LYDIA. Not yet. But there are some lovely churches in Switzerland.

PAUL. Yes and you can ski all the way down the aisle. ...I still think our marriage should have worked. Nicole does too.

LYDIA. Oh, stop it – that's a lie. It was chaos. The whole thing was absurd.

PAUL. Absurd, yes, but passionate. Oh God – so much passion!

LYDIA. And that was why it was so chaotic. It was nothing *but* passion. It was exhausting! Passion is all very exciting for a moment or two, but you have to have a break occasionally. I never got any shopping done! Do you have any idea what it's like to be behind on your sleep for seven years?

PAUL. I do. It's glorious. ...Is he rich?

LYDIA. Who?

PAUL. Is he?

LYDIA. I don't have to answer any of your questions. You're on *my* territory. So now you need to leave. I have to change.

PAUL. You'll never change. *(He stands)* And I hope this "Charles" knows that. ...Goodbye, Lydia.

LYDIA. Yes, yes. Careful the door doesn't hit you in the back on your way out.

PAUL. Not even a quick kiss?

LYDIA. I know where your lips have been – I'm not going near them.

PAUL. Not even for old time's sake.

LYDIA. If I do – just for old time's sake - then will you go?

PAUL. Absolutely. Promise.

*(**LYDIA** stands and offers herself to be kissed. **PAUL** leans in to kiss her. At the last moment, she turns her head, so that the kiss lands on her cheek)*

PAUL. Either you just turned your head, or my aim's getting very bad.

LYDIA. I don't suppose these days you have much chance for target practice?

*(**PAUL** grabs her with both hands and forces a kiss onto her lips. Affronted, **LYDIA** pushes him off)*

How dare you! Forcing yourself on me. I shall call the police!

PAUL. Ah, yes, the Love Police. But they're never around when you need them.

LYDIA. You're a disgrace!

PAUL. Yes, I know. *(Laughing)*

LYDIA. I'm glad you find it all so amusing. Our relationship always was a joke to you.

PAUL. Not true. But it did always put a smile on my face. We had happy days…didn't we?

LYDIA. I suppose we had our moments.

PAUL. We certainly did. …I bet you still think about us every day.

LYDIA. No, I don't! You're so arrogant. I've had all kinds of lovers – many of whom would put you in the shade.

PAUL. Oh, I think that's highly unlikely.

(He grabs her and kisses her again. She pulls away in fury and slaps him across the face)

LYDIA. Get off me!

PAUL. Would you mind also slapping the other side, I don't want to leave here with my face lob-sided.

(She duly slaps his other cheek)

…Thank you. That's much better.

(He kisses her again. She pushes him off again.)

LYDIA. I have a performance to do!

PAUL. So do I!

(They now grab each other and kiss passionately and with abandon. They stagger across the room as they ravage each other. PAUL manages to force out a few words)

PAUL. Those slaps really hurt by the way. ...I may have lost a tooth...

(Unfooted by the various blooms scattered around, they tumble together onto the floor and on top of all the flowers. Various noises and yelps orchestrate the physical action in amongst the blooms. During this, there is a knock on the door which they ignore. Then a moment later, it opens and MARGARET looks in)

MARGARET. Time is getting on, so I thought I should pass on the director's notes. Lydia? *(She now sees the commotion on the floor. Not knowing how to react, she just takes out her notebook and, as quietly as she can, tears out the page with LYDIA's notes on it. She then reaches in to place the note on her dressing table. She then leaves, closing the door behind her.)*

LYDIA. No...No! This is not the time – I have a – this is ridiculous!

PAUL. I like ridiculous. Viva ridiculous!

LYDIA. No – stop. Stop!

(She gets up from the floor, weak kneed and with flower petals in her hair)

You've ruined my lovely flowers! I can't... - This is why the marriage never worked. You have no boundaries.

(PAUL sits up. His shirt open, hair ruffled)

PAUL. Oh to hell with boundaries.

LYDIA. I can't do this – I have a show to do! - I mean - I have a fiancé! I have a fiancé and a show to do.

PAUL. And I still love you.

LYDIA. You don't! Stop! You love the actress, Paul. That's all. It's all it ever was. And I'm not the actress any more.

PAUL. *(Laughing)* But that's the thing. You are. And always will be. You can run away from the theatre, but it'll get a map and hunt you down.

LYDIA. That's where you're wrong. I'm finished. Finished with all of it. I want a – a simple life.

PAUL. Boring! Dull!

LYDIA. You've not been here these past ten years. You only remember it as it was. And yes, it was wonderful - sometimes, but… Oh, I don't have to explain. You'd never understand.

PAUL. What the hell are you doing? Moving to Switzerland? Your heartbeat is here, Lydia.

LYDIA. It's different now. Something has to change.

PAUL. What kind of change is that? Diving under the sheets with some rich old sod from Zurich.

LYDIA. Geneva! He's a rich old sod from Geneva! - And he's not a sod. But rich – yes. He has more money than I could make in a hundred years treading on that stage.

PAUL. But you'll happily spend that hundred years. Maybe you *will* enjoy it for a while. But come back! You're crazy if you don't come back. This is your entire world.

LYDIA. Yes, it has been. But now …

PAUL. What?

LYDIA. *(A pause)* Now that world is pushing me away. I love it – you know how much I - …Yes, when you have it in your grasp, it's still wonderful. …But the waiting. The waiting kills me.

*(**LYDIA** sits)*

PAUL. Sorry, I just don't understand.

LYDIA. Of course you don't. You're on the outside looking in. You don't see the whole scenario. …What you fail to realise is this - They don't write parts for us. For us women. Once we reach a certain age. …There are just a handful of roles and you have to wait for the call. While these younger actresses rush from one stage to the next, the mature, older actress just has to wait. I use to run like they did. Run from rehearsal to a show, from interview to concert. Running, rushing, out of breath. And it was exhilarating. And then autumn comes... and you find yourself – lost, impatient... Wondering if you're perhaps now forgotten. Fearing that you actually are. ...And eventually you get a role, of course I get a role, I'm Lydia Martin. The great star. But so clearly fading now because I had to wait for it. Wait for so long that the interval nearly killed me. And so however grand the work is when it finally comes, it's not enough. It doesn't wipe the fear away.

PAUL. And living by a lake, staring at the view – you think that will be enough?

LYDIA. At least it fulfils its expectations. ...And I think it will be beautiful.

(She looks at herself in the mirror)

...I'm so tired, Paul.

PAUL. The tireless Lydia. Finally beaten.

LYDIA. Not beaten. Just retreating.

(She starts re-touching her hair)

Oh god, my hair! I look like I've fallen into a hedge.

PAUL. You've never looked better.

*(**LYDIA** turns to him, a little smile)*

LYDIA. It's time to go. I mean – really.

PAUL. Alright. But dinner. Tomorrow. Delay your trip 24 hours.

LYDIA. No.

PAUL. With Nicole. Bring Nicole. The three of us. One last time.

LYDIA. Paul – just say Goodbye.

*(**PAUL** gets up and goes to the door)*

PAUL. No – I won't. I refuse.

(At this moment, KATHERINE returns. She is carrying an old jar with the flower stalks in it)

…They look so much lovelier now that you've displayed them.

KATHERINE. Lydia – ten minutes.

LYDIA. Yes - thank you. Put those here on my table.

(KATHERINE puts the jar on LYDIA's dressing table)

KATHERINE. You've got another visitor, but really we shouldn't let any more back now. We'll be late going up.

LYDIA. Who is it? Not another lover. *(To paul)* I'm tired of lovers.

KATHERINE. No - it's your agent.

LYDIA. Oh for goodness sake!

KATHERINE. Yes, that's what I said. But she's very keen to see you.

LYDIA. She always is. Alright – I suppose that's fine. But tell her she has to be brief - I'm not even changed yet.

KATHERINE. Yes, of course.

LYDIA. And we need a new hair stocking.

(KATHERINE nods and exits to speak to HARRIET outside of the door)

KATHERINE. *(Off)* She doesn't have much time, so please keep it short, if you wouldn't mind.

HARRIET. *(Off)* Of course, of course.

(HARRIET enters. She is carrying a bottle of brandy)

HARRIET. Here she is! Brava! Brava!

LYDIA. Harriet, how lovely to see you. And you've come armed with alcohol. Even lovelier.

(Kissing of various cheeks ensues and the bottle is placed on the table)

HARRIET. The least I could do. Honestly, I really didn't know what to get you. Flowers are so predictable. I thought some Swiss Chocolate would be funny. But then I thought "Oh Harriet that's not funny at all" and so I didn't bring it because most of my clients aren't funny, including the comedians, and the last thing we need on top of that is an un-funny agent. But here's brandy instead. ...Sorry, I think I'm a bit flustered. Am I even making sense? It's just such an emotional night.

LYDIA. I'm trying not to think too much about it. Do you remember Paul? My ex husband? He was just leaving.

HARRIET. Paul, yes. What are you up to these days?

PAUL. Just leaving, apparently.

LYDIA. *(To* **HARRIET***)* Would you like a little drink? *(Looking at the label on the brandy bottle)* Perhaps some of this thoughtful, but inexpensive, brandy you've bought me?

HARRIET. A brandy, yes – very nice.

LYDIA. Would you do the honours?

HARRIET. Of course.

PAUL. Let me help you.

HARRIET. Thank you.

(**HARRIET** *and* **PAUL** *find some glasses and pours three brandies, while* **LYDIA** *continues with her make-up)*

(To paul) ...It's such an extraordinary evening. I go to lots of important theatre events, as you can imagine, but this is quite different. I'm very nervous. Some shows are very bad, of course, but you can't say anything about that to anybody, which is just terrible. I always have to go backstage and earn my ten percent – and I wish they could somehow drag me away. I need a giant hook or something. But I go and say all these wonderful things to all these awful actors regardless of what horror has just scarred my eyes.

(They take a glass of brandy each)

…After my many years in the business, I feel now that if an actor is bad – we should just tell them so. It can only be helpful information. Otherwise they're all going to go around for the rest of their lives *thinking* they're wonderful when that's not the truth. And that's quite dangerous for all these theatre productions. I mean, I don't want to get in a car with someone who *thinks* they're a good driver – I want a good driver, if you see what I mean. Otherwise we could end up skidding off the road and being burned alive. If you see what I mean? Accidents should be avoided, not encouraged. Anyway – *(raising her glass)* Cheers!

(LYDIA and HARRIET take a sip of their brandy. PAUL drinks his in one gulp)

PAUL. That's horrible! Very nasty. I think I'll have another.

(He pours himself another brandy)

LYDIA. I thought you were leaving.

PAUL. Oh, I'm leaving alright. Just one for the road.

(He drinks his second large brandy in one gulp)

PAUL. Farewell, then.

LYDIA. At last!

PAUL. Another quick kiss, perhaps?

(LYDIA has had enough of him. She gets up from her chair and physically shoves PAUL out of the door)

(From beyond the door) …I'll take that as a "no".

(LYDIA slams the door shut)

HARRIET. *(Chuckling)* He hasn't lost his charm.

LYDIA. No. We should find a surgeon and have it removed.

HARRIET. It's nice that you stayed friends.

LYDIA. We didn't. I don't know what he thinks he's doing here. …Oh, Harriet, it's such a strange night. Everybody's come out of the woodwork. There are flowers here from all kinds of people – from *years* ago. People I've loved, hated, admired, and in many cases, deliberately forgotten. I don't like how it makes me feel. I feel exposed. I should have gone quietly.

HARRIET. No – never. Make a splash. You always did that so well.

(**LYDIA** *sits back at her dressing table*)

… I don't know what I shall do after you've gone. You're my only major star. I have other clients, of course, but – oh, they're all such talentless fools.

LYDIA. Harriet!

HARRIET. It's true! I don't mean to be insulting - not *all* of them are in both categories. Some are talentless, and others are fools. But they do seem to be either one or the other. I'm such a terrible agent. I pick all the wrong people. Apart from you. I'm not very well designed for that side of the business. Maybe I should have become a playwright?

LYDIA. Now you're getting hysterical. Drink your brandy.

(**HARRIET** *drinks a little more of her brandy as instructed*)

HARRIET. Forgive me. You make me very nervous.

LYDIA. Why?

HARRIET. You make everybody nervous. You knew that, didn't you? You should be proud of it. That's how you know when you're a true star – when everybody panics in your presence. And you truly are a star, Lydia. For one more night, anyway. …I shall miss you enormously. I don't mind telling you that. And I don't just mean the commission. Agents aren't only interested in commission. Despite the rumours! *(A little laugh)* No – we care for the *real* talent. Fall a little bit in love with our finest people. I suppose, if it comes down to it, we're all frustrated performers ourselves, deep inside. Well, not so deep. And we live our dreams through our clients – through you. You make us part of it - this magic box. And it won't be the same. I'm sorry to say. …Although – I did get a very interesting offer for you this morning, which – if you wanted, we could discuss over lunch on Monday?

LYDIA. I'll be in Geneva. No more Mondays, Harriet.

HARRIET. Well – just thought I'd mention it, in case…? …I mean, you can't be persuaded…?

LYDIA. I've thought about this for many years.

HARRIET. I know you have.

LYDIA. It's all about timing. I don't want to be one of those old actresses who only appears in public when somebody dies, who only gets to deliver speeches at funerals. There are too many of us. I want to leave at the top. Or at a point from where I can still see the view. …But I shall miss it. All of it. I'll even miss you.

HARRIET. Don't - you'll make me cry.

LYDIA. Careful, Harriet. You don't want all those other producers to know you have a heart. They'll eat you alive.

HARRIET. Oh dear, oh dear. Do you have a tissue? At some point I think I'm going to need one.

(**LYDIA** *gives her a tissue. She goes to sit on the sofa and blows her nose*)

…It's very comfortable. The sofa.

LYDIA. I had it brought from home. It's an old one, but it does the trick.

HARRIET. Is it going to Switzerland with you?

LYDIA. No, I thought I might leave it. For whoever comes along and steps into my shoes, takes over my room and mirror. It will be the sofa for the next rising star – the next great actress. So the *bitch* can be comfortable. (*A wry chuckle*) …Where was it you first saw me, Harriet? I've forgotten.

HARRIET. "Hedda Gabler".

LYDIA. Oh yes. I wasn't very good.

HARRIET. Not good!? You were spectacular.

LYDIA. No, I wasn't. …Was I?

HARRIET. You were a marvel. The whole world opened up to you after that run. I had to fight to represent you. Yes! Everyone in town was after you. ...But I got you in the end. And for all these wonderful years. You did far more for my career than I could ever have done for yours. And that's the truth of it. You earned me – respect. "That's Lydia Martin's agent", they would say. And they would nod politely. Before then, I was just nobody, really. Always hanging around backstage – like an old sofa. I have so much to be grateful for. To be grateful to you for...

(She starts to cry)

LYDIA. Oh, Harriet... Take the whole box.

(She throws the whole box of tissues to **HARRIET** *and she wipes her eyes)*

...Can't you spare some of those tears for the curtain call? A bit of open weeping amongst the audience is always terribly effective.

HARRIET. I'll do my best.

LYDIA. If you could. ...Do you have a cigarette?

HARRIET. I do, yes.

(She takes a pack of cigarettes from her pocket and removes one)

LYDIA. Light it and blow it at me.

HARRIET. What?

LYDIA. Harriet, you know perfectly well I *don't* smoke. And I've no intention of starting again, it took me *years* to give up. But if you could just –

HARRIET. *(Taking out a box of matches, confused)* You want me to - ?

LYDIA. Light the bloody cigarette and blow the smoke in my face. I would have thought it was obvious!

HARRIET. Alright – just a second -

((HARRIET *lights a cigarette and blows the smoke into* **LYDIA**'s *face as requested.* **LYDIA** *breathes it the smoke*

deeply. **NICOLE** *returns, dismayed by the ritual. The smoke blowing is repeated)*

NICOLE. Oh for pity's sake, mother, just have a bloody cigarette.

LYDIA. I gave up smoking, Nicole. And I'm not backing down. That's your generation's problem – you have no will power. *(To* **HARRIET***)* Blow harder.

*(***HARRIET*** awkwardly blows more smoke into* **LYDIA***'s face)*

NICOLE. I thought I'd quickly pop in again because some annoying man said we had to all clear out now. He said you're going to be late.

LYDIA. What man?

NICOLE. The one with the clip-board.

LYDIA. He's the stage manager. It's his job to make sure we go up on time. And my job to make sure we don't.

NICOLE. Well – anyway…

*(***HARRIET*** blows more smoke)*

NICOLE. …So I'll see you afterwards?

LYDIA. Come back at the interval.

NICOLE. Won't you be busy?

LYDIA. Never too busy to see you, my angel. Never, never.

*(***HARRIET*** blows more smoke)*

NICOLE. *(To* **HARRIET***)* Could you stop doing that now? It's like trying to talk to my mother through fog.

LYDIA. Actually, you can accompany Harriet downstairs. Before she uses up all my tissues. I shall need them.

(She gestures to the tissue box on the sofa. **NICOLE** *retrieves it for her)*

HARRIET. Sorry, yes. An emotional night.

LYDIA. So – see you both later.

NICOLE. *(To* **HARRIET***)* This way, then. I'll show you the short cut.

HARRIET. *(To* **LYDIA***)* Goodbye, my wonderful Lydia.

(She kisses **LYDIA** *on the cheek.* **LYDIA** *whispers in her ear)*

LYDIA. *(Whispered)* Leave the cigarette.

*(***HARRIET** *leaves the cigarette behind and then* **NICOLE** *escorts her out of the door.* **LYDIA** *is now alone in the room. She takes one deep drag on the cigarette and then stubs it out. She sprays perfume around the room. She then picks up her telephone and dials the stage door)*

LYDIA. *(When her call is answered)* …Is Katherine nearby? … Send her up. - And no more visitors. However keen they are.

(She hangs up the phone. She then puts some opera music on to play, something classical, gentle, an aria by a great soprano. She dims the lights in the room. And then uses the music to enforce relaxation and to focus herself. Shortly, **KATHERINE** *enters. She is carrying a new hair stocking. Though* **LYDIA** *is standing with her eyes shut, she senses that* **KATHERINE** *is there)*

…*(Above the music)* Let's get on with this.

(With the operatic aria continuing to play, **KATHERINE** *fetches* **LYDIA***'s costume dress and prepares it ready for her to step into.* **LYDIA** *removes some of her own clothing and then* **KATHERINE** *carefully puts the dress on to her and buttons it up. This done,* **LYDIA** *sits at her table and* **KATHERINE** *takes a hair stocking and places it over* **LYDIA***'s head. She then takes the wig and puts that on. As she adjusts the wig, the lights fade to blackout.)*

End of Scene One

Scene Two

(The music continues as lights rise on the second area to the side of the dressing room set. This is the stage of the theatre, where we will watch a short scene from Chekhov's "The Cherry Orchard". There is the suggestion of a stage setting for this Russian play – a chair, table, a large vase. **LYDIA** *takes the role of "**LUBOV** ranevskaya".)*

(The performance is presented facing upstage so that the actors have their backs to the actual audience. We therefore see the actors lit in silhouette and we observe the footlights at the furthest point upstage and poiting towards us. Perhaps a flat or backcloth gives a sense of the auditorium in the blackness beyond. The other roles in the play are taken by the actors who play **CHARLES** *(in the role of* **LOPAKHIN***, a merchant) and* **PAUL** *(in the role of* **GAEV***,* **LUBOV***'s brother). We never fully see the men's faces. All characters are dimly lit on stage apart from* **LUBOV/LYDIA***. The scene is adapted from act two of "The Cherry Orchard" –)*

LOPAKHIN. You must forgive my saying this, but I don't believe I have ever met such frivolous people like you before, or anyone who is so un-professional in business and so generally peculiar. Here I am explaining in simple and clear language that you must leave your estate, lease all of the land without delay. And yet you look at me blankly as though nothing I've said has registered at all.

LUBOV. What on earth do you expect me to say? Tell us, what on earth are we supposed to do?

LOPAKHIN. I tell you, each and every day. I say the exact thing, the same thing, every single day. Both the cherry orchard and all your land must be leased off and at once, immediately – you must go to auction. This is the unavoidable certainty that is staring at you. Tell me you understand! Once you make up your minds, once you decide – finally - then you'll have all the money you want, in abundance, and you'll be saved from imminent disaster.

LUBOV. But they will lease the land to these terrible common people who rent villas - it's so vulgar. That's what it is – vulgar!

GAEV. I agree with you, absolutely. Vulgar!

LOPAKHIN. Don't you hear me! Must I scream it at the top of my lungs? Or should I just burst into tears and fall to the ground in a faint. This is unbearable. Such ignorance, such arrogance. I can't stand it! You're too much to bear! *(To* **GAEV***)* You silly old woman!

GAEV. How dare you! What a thing to say!

LOPAKHIN. Silly, *stupid,* old woman! I give up on you. I abandon you to your fate! *(He heads for the exit)*

*(***LYDIA** *(as* **LUBOV***) now turns to look across the stage at* **LOPAKHIN***. So that now we see her face in profile.)*

•**LUBOV.** *(Frightened)* No! Stop – please! Don't go away. *(A yell)* Please! *(***LOPAKHIN** *stops)* Perhaps there is some other way?

LOPAKHIN. What's the good of trying to help you!

LUBOV. Please – stay a while. It's nicer when you're here. Don't abandon me. I'm terribly frightened. I feel as if the house will at any moment collapse on top of us, crush us all. Have we been too sinful? Is this our punishment? ...Oh, the sins of my life. ...I've always thrown money around without discipline, without thought, like a woman truly mad and with no thought of the consequences. I took as my husband a man who came to my arms laden with debts. He died of love. A love for champagne and excess. He drank terribly - and I took his sin and made another out of it. I fell in love with another man, and I went off with him. And just as it happened – I received the first punishment of my sin, coming like a hammer blow to my head. Here, in this dark river...my boy was drowned. I ran away, as far as I could, running, weeping, never to return here, never to see this river again. ...I closed my eyes and ran aimlessly, wildly. But *he* followed me…without pity for me, without respecting my need to be alone. I bought a villa for us and then his illness began. For three years I knew no peace either by day or night. The sickness of this man wore me out entirely, dried up my very soul. A year ago, the villa was sold to pay our debts. No sooner was this done, when he abandoned me for another woman. I took poison. What else should I do? But an act so shameful… When I recovered, my thoughts were only of Russia. To return here. To my land… *(she wipes her tears)* Lord, dear God be merciful to me, forgive me for my sins! I beg that you punish me no more!

(Some klezmer music can be heard in the distance, played by a small jewish band of violins, etc)

…Do I hear music? *(She listens)*

GAEV. It is our celebrated Jewish band. Do you remember?

LUBOV. They still play together? Oh how wonderful it would be if they came here one evening to play for us. To calm my soul.

LOPAKHIN. It reminds me. Did I tell you? I saw a terribly funny play last night at the theatre.

LUBOV. At the theatre? I'm certain it was not funny at all. You should not go and watch these plays. Your time would be better spent taking a good look at yourself. At the greyness of your life.

(The lights now dim on the stage scene and we fade up the sound of an audience applauding rapturously.)

End of Scene Two

Scene Three

(The theatre stage area disappears and we are back in the dressing room. It is interval. Lights rise on the room as **KATHERINE** *enters. She prepares everything for* **LYDIA**'*s return – a drink, a towel, some throat spray, perfume, etc. The audience applause can be heard in the distance. Momentarily,* **LYDIA** *enters, elated)*

LYDIA. Thunderous! Did you hear it?

KATHERINE. Yes, it was – oh, it was amazing.

(The applause now comes to an end)

LYDIA. I've never heard applause like it. They're taking the roof off! Oh look at me – I'm shaking.

KATHERINE. Sit down – catch your breath.

*(***KATHERINE*** gives ***LYDIA*** a small towel to wipe her brow)*

LYDIA. Has there ever been a night like this? Has there?

KATHERINE. Never.

LYDIA. Wonderful. Wonderful!

KATHERINE. I'm sure you can't wait to get back out there.

LYDIA. No! I don't want to go back out. I want to bottle tonight right now – just as it is. And run away. It's going so well that all there is left for us to do is mess it up. ...Have you made some tea?

*(***KATHERINE*** brings over a cup of herbal tea)*

KATHERINE. It's still a little hot. *(She blows on it)*

LYDIA. Well, well. Such a night. *(Looking in the mirror)* I look ten years younger all of a sudden. Glowing. Like a new bride. *(She drinks some tea)* Oh – it is a little hot.

*(***KATHERINE*** takes the cup back and blows on it more. As she does so,* **LYDIA** *notices the company manager's note on the table.)*

LYDIA. What's this?

KATHERINE. A few notes from your director.

*(**LYDIA** laughs mockingly and then starts folding it up into a paper aeroplane.)*

LYDIA. That man is quite ridiculous.

(A knock on the door)

…Only come in if you're charming!

(A pause. The door does not open)

MARGARET. *(From outside of the door)* …It's Margaret.

LYDIA. Well, come in anyway.

*(**MARGARET** enters, smiling, notebook in hand)*

MARGARET. What a night!

LYDIA. Yes. Yes!

MARGARET. Roger is very pleased. He wanted you to know that so far he's very satisfied. And - did you get his notes?

LYDIA. I did. Duck!

*(At this point she throws the paper aeroplane at **MARGARET**. She ducks and it flies by)*

Did you see them all stand up? It was just the end of the Act. I've never seen that before. It's a night for the history books. *(To **KATHERINE**)* How long do we have?

KATHERINE. Just over ten minutes.

LYDIA. I must make sure I nap for a few minutes. It helps me focus.

*(**MARGARET** sits on the sofa. **LYDIA** takes out her powder puff compact and touches up her make up)*

MARGARET. So - the second half. Roger has some ideas.

LYDIA. And what does that have to do with me?

MARGARET. The rehearsal never ends, that's what Roger says - we must always keep improving.

LYDIA. I told you that you shouldn't have slept with him. Now you believe every stupid thing he comes out with.

MARGARET. I happen to agree.

LYDIA. Oh what's the point, Margaret? In an hour or so, I'm packing my last bag for Geneva. Improving my craft is no longer of any interest to me. Did you hear that applause? Did you?

MARGARET. Yes I did.

LYDIA. And? *(MARGARET has no response) (more forcefully)* … And?

MARGARET. Lydia, I don't –

LYDIA. *(Ferocious)* And!!??

MARGARET. *(Realising)* Oh – *and* you were wonderful.

LYDIA. Thank you!

(She slams her compact down on to the table, exasperated)

Honestly, the effort you have to put in to get a compliment around here. …Where's my drink?

(KATHERINE passes her the tea again)

…No, not that! The other one.

(KATHERINE passes her the brandy and a glass. LYDIA pours herself a large brandy)

LYDIA. You know, Margaret, you have a special talent. You can suck all the joy and energy out of a room in a matter of seconds. Not many people can do that. You should join a circus.

MARGARET. I'm just doing my job.

LYDIA. Your job – and Roger's too - is to support the leading lady.

MARGARET. That's not true. His job is to direct the show, whether it supports you or not. And it's not easy. He finds it very difficult.

LYDIA. Only because he doesn't know what he's doing. He'd have more success directing traffic. This company of actors knows how to do their job. Anton Chekhov has provided the dialogue, Mary the costumes, and that strange man who keeps falling asleep has designed the set. Roger's contribution is to simply say "lovely" or "getting there" depending on how the mood takes him. That is not directing - that is mumbling useless comments. And if there's anything negative to be said, he hides in the bar while his mistress passes notes around. He lurks in the shadows. I wonder sometimes if he actually exists. During week two of rehearsal there was a day when we got half way through Act One before anybody even realized that neither of you had turned up!

MARGARET. That wasn't our fault. The taxi got lost.

LYDIA. So did your careers.

MARGARET. Lydia! I have never been so insulted.

LYDIA. Oh, of course you have! And those are just the things that people have said to your face! If you heard the rest of it, you'd faint. Now please take your notebook and go bother somebody else. Talk to Michael – his voice is horribly rough and croaky out there tonight. The audience is very confused. They think his character has been possessed by the devil.

*(At this moment, **CHARLES** stumbles in through the door, out of breath and unsteady)*

LYDIA. Charles! What are you doing here?

CHARLES. …When did they add all those extra stairs?

LYDIA. You'll give yourself a heart attack. Come and sit down.

CHARLES. No, no – I have to turn right around. If I don't start heading back now, I'll miss the second half.

LYDIA. Then why did you come?

CHARLES. I wanted to see you. I'm in love with you. Did you forget?

LYDIA. How could I? You silly, silly, lovely man. You at least have time for a drink?

CHARLES. A drink? No, I need to concentrate on breathing. I just felt absolutely compelled to come and tell you how simply wonderful you were.

LYDIA. You could have telephoned.

CHARLES. But then I wouldn't get a kiss.

LYDIA. Oh, you silly, silly, lovely -

(She gives him an affectionate kiss and embrace)

CHARLES. You're a precious jewel. I could stay in your arms forever. *(A brief pause)* ...Right, I must be off.

LYDIA. Oh Charles!

CHARLES. The second half. I don't want to miss a second of it. Will they sell the Orchard? Won't they? It's gripping.

LYDIA. Let Katherine help you. The stairs are very steep.

*(**LYDIA** beckons her forward and **KATHERINE** goes to help him on his way)*

CHARLES. *(To **KATHERINE**)* We should hurry.

LYDIA. You've got seven minutes. You'll be fine.

CHARLES. *(Seeing **MARGARET**)* Who's this?

LYDIA. That's Margaret. She makes occasional appearances on behalf of Roger.

CHARLES. *(Suspicious)* Roger? Who is this Roger? Another ex-lover?

LYDIA. He's the director! And actresses of my standing *never* sleep with their directors. It's very unprofessional. And in my experience, no help to your career at all. ...I'll see you after the show. Wait downstairs.

*(**KATHERINE** exits with **CHARLES**. **CHARLES** blows her a kiss as he goes)*

MARGARET. ...So that was your Charles?

LYDIA. Yes. My husband to be.

MARGARET. What time are you flying with him to Geneva tomorrow?

LYDIA. At 11am.

MARGARET. Maybe you should go at 10am – he looks like he might not last that long.

*(**MARGARET** laughs at her own joke, but **LYDIA** is unfuriated. She throws her glass of brandy in **MARGARET**'s face)*

Lydia! How dare you! - Give me a towel.

LYDIA. I'm not giving you one of my towels – you'll steal it as a souvenir.

MARGARET. You're absurd!

(**MARGARET** *heads angrily for the door*)

I hope - …I hope you forget your lines, bump into the furniture and – and fall into the orchestra pit! - Wig first!

(*She exits, loudly slamming the door behind her.* **LYDIA** *pauses for a moment, chuckling to herself*)

LYDIA. …Oh I shall miss the camaraderie of the theatre.

(*She quickly checks herself in the mirror and then picks up the phone to call the stage door*)

(*When the call is answered*) …How long do I have? …Tell Katherine to come and get me at the last minute.

(*She puts the phone down and prepares to take a quick nap. She dims the lights, curls up on the sofa, and closes her eyes. After a moment, in the semi darkness, the door opens.* **NICOLE** *comes in quietly*)

NICOLE. It's me.

LYDIA. Come in, come in. I can talk, but I must keep my eyes shut.

NICOLE. I passed Charles on the stairs. You know it might be quicker to lower him down on a rope.

LYDIA. Don't be rude.

NICOLE. And there was also an angry woman that smelt of brandy.

LYDIA. That was the company manager. They all turn to drink eventually. (*She pats the side of the sofa*) Come and sit.

(**NICOLE** *duly sits on the floor by the sofa, close to* **LYDIA.** **LYDIA** *affectionately plays with her hair*)

LYDIA. (*After a moment*) …Nicole.

NICOLE. Yes mother?

LYDIA. …Wash your hair. It's too greasy.

NICOLE. I've been too busy today. But I promise I'll wash it before I come to Switzerland.

LYDIA. That's probably months away. You'll be able to fry bacon on it by then. …But you *are* coming?

NICOLE. Yes, I'll come.

LYDIA. I *want* you to come. I shall miss you. …It's very lovely there. Tall trees and rolling hillsides. And the snow. So much snow. The whiteness is pure and perfect. That's what I want my life to be. Not the disaster I've so often made of everything.

NICOLE. Don't be silly. You've had a marvelous career.

LYDIA. I would have given it all up for a *normal* family life. Sunday lunch. Christmas day. Long walks. Endless, pointless conversations by the fire. I'm sorry you didn't have all that. Children need a stable home life. They need to see a mother and father together, in love, otherwise how do they know what life should be?

NICOLE. I didn't miss it. I quite liked all the chaos. Visiting you one week, dad the next. Never knowing where I was going. All those different beds. It certainly keeps you on your toes.

LYDIA. Have *you* found anyone? To love, I mean – to be with?

NICOLE. You don't have to worry about me.

LYDIA. But I do worry. After tomorrow, I won't be here to look after you.

NICOLE. Mother – you have never been here to look after me. The day I broke my hand at school, you were doing an interview. When I failed my examinations, you were busy collecting an award. And when I first had my heart broken, you were on tour as Lady Bracknell.

LYDIA. When did you have your heart broken?

NICOLE. I was eleven. His name was James. He was much older than me. Twelve, at least. I was very upset. I didn't know what I should do.

LYDIA. You should have washed your hair for starters.

(NICOLE *slaps her mother's hand, affronted*)

(*After a brief pause*) I'm sorry I wasn't there.

NICOLE. That's alright. Strangely, I think James works in the theatre now.

LYDIA. Really? Get me his full name, I'll have him killed.

NICOLE. Let's not be too dramatic. I did get over it.

LYDIA. Maybe you didn't. Deep down in your soul. Maybe that's why you're still on your own…?

NICOLE. I'm not on my own.

(LYDIA *opens her eyes and looks at* NICOLE)

LYDIA. You're not? Tell me more.

NICOLE. …No, mother. It's delicate. And you tend to break things…

(KATHERINE *quietly comes back in*)

KATHERINE. …It's time.

LYDIA. Oh dear. And still so much to say.

(NICOLE *stands up*)

NICOLE. I'll leave you to it. See you at the end.

(NICOLE *leaves, touching her hair as she goes to check its greasiness.* LYDIA *sits up*)

KATHERINE. She's so nice.

LYDIA. Yes. How on earth did I manage that?

(KATHERINE *now turns up the lights to full. Then she sits beside* LYDIA *on the sofa*)

KATHERINE. Look at me for a second.

(LYDIA*s turns her head to* KATHERINE *and she straightens her wig*)

…That's better. Well? Are you ready to bring the house down? For one last time?

LYDIA. One last time.

(LYDIA *stands up.* KATHERINE *fetches a large fur coat, additional costume for the next act of the show. She puts the coat on* LYDIA. *When this is done,* LYDIA *affectionately touches* KATHERINE*'s cheek)*

LYDIA. Thank you.

(*She leans in and gives* KATHERINE *a kiss)*

You're the only person working in this building who likes me. I'm beginning to think I'm not very nice.

KATHERINE. They don't pay you to be nice. They pay you to be an actress. Take a deep breath. They're all waiting for you. And you can't disappoint them.

(*Lights cross-fade to the "stage" area to the side of the dressing room.* LYDIA *walks on to the stage set, wrapping the fur coat tightly around her. It is night time. The room is cold and dimly lit. The klezmer music is heard again in the distance.* LUBOV/LYDIA *stands at the middle of the scene, looking around the room, contemplating her future. After a moment, the lights and music slowly fade out.*)

End of Act One

ACT TWO

Scene One

(On "the stage". A second excerpt from "The Cherry Orchard" in the same setting as the first scene. **LYDIA** *playing* **LUBOV**, *the* **CHARLES** *actor as* **LOPAKHIN**, *the* **PAUL** *actor as* **GAEV**. *The performances played facing upstage, except for* **LYDIA** *who is regularly caught in profile)*

LUBOV. I'll wait sitting here for a moment more. It's as though I had never truly noticed what the walls and ceilings of this house were really like. I've never even glanced at them for more than a moment. And yet now I find myself looking at them so greedily, devouring them, and feeling such tenderness and love…

GAEV. I remember, I must have been about six years old, and one Trinity Sunday, I sat at this very window, I can see it now so clearly, watching my father going to church…

LUBOV. Has everything been packed away?

LOPAKHIN. Yes, everything has gone, I think.

LUBOV. And we shall be gone too, not even a human soul remaining behind.

LOPAKHIN. Until springtime.

GAEV. *(Deeply moved, almost in tears)* The train…the station…

LUBOV. Come – it's time – we must go!

LOPAKHIN. Yes! Until the spring. Until we are together again!

*(***LOPAKHIN*** exits.* **LUBOV** *and* **GAEV** *are left alone. They fall into each other's arms and sob restrainedly and quietly, fearing that somebody might hear them. In*

47

this embrace, which is maintained through the following dialogue, GAEV *faces upstage and* LUBOV/LYDIA *faces downstage)*

GAEV. *(In despair)* My sister, oh my sister...

LUBOV. And so we stare at these walls and windows for the final time... My mother would love to walk so gently and silently around this room...

GAEV. My sister, my sister!

LUBOV. My dead, my sweet, my beautiful orchard! My life, my youth, my happiness... Goodbye... Goodbye!

(Lights fade out on the scene and gently rise on the dressing room)

Scene Two

(**KATHERINE** *is alone in the dressing room, tidying things up and sipping a hot drink.* **NICOLE** *enters. She is surprised to see her*)

KATHERINE. What are you doing here? Aren't you watching?

NICOLE. I've seen it. I know how it ends. They get rid of the orchard. Finally. After three hours.

KATHERINE. But it's your mother's last performance.

NICOLE. And it's my mother I'm interested in. Not the performance.

(**KATHERINE** *looks bemused*)

…Katherine, it's not important, it's only a bloody play!

(**KATHERINE** *quickly shuts the door as though she has said something terrible*)

KATHERINE. Keep your voice down. The actors will tear your throat out if they hear you say that.

(**NICOLE** *laughs*)

I know a play doesn't seem important to us. But to them - It's like the world will come to an end if they don't get it right. They really *feel* it. Never underestimate how much it means to these people.

NICOLE. You've been working in theatres far too long.

KATHERINE. You think I don't know that? … I suppose you want a drink? The kettle's hot. I can pour you a herbal tea.

NICOLE. That sounds hideous.

KATHERINE. It's good for you. (*She prepares the drink*)

NICOLE. …So what do you do when she's – you know – not here.

KATHERINE. Tidy a bit, relax. Eat a few of her chocolates. Then re-organize them so she doesn't notice.

NICOLE. Can't you go out?

KATHERINE. No! What if something happens? A torn dress, a broken ankle, a dislodged wig. I'm on standby like the fire brigade. ...Actually, I rather like being here in the room. Once everybody's gone. Some people like empty theatres – you know, with just a single ghost light and rows of empty seats. But I like an empty dressing room. The calm before the storm. *(She passing* **NICOLE** *her drink)*

NICOLE. Thank you.

KATHERINE. Don't thank me till you've tasted it.

(**NICOLE** *takes a sip and pulls a face)*

...Your mother drinks it to make her relax.

NICOLE. So it tastes bad *and* it doesn't work. *(She sits)* ... What will you do then? Next week when mother's up the Alps.

KATHERINE. Another show. Another actress.

NICOLE. Is it that easy?

KATHERINE. Once you've worked with Lydia Martin you're a little more in demand. Some other spoiled "grand dame" will be waiting for me to run her errands and put up with her abuse. But still somehow I love it. I like to care for them, help them do their job. And I like that I can save them with a few casual words of encouragement. There are many occasions when the show would absolutely not have gone on if the dresser hadn't said the right thing at the right moment. We always keep a few compliments on standby. Ready to pull out of the hat when the screaming begins. I find all that hysteria really invigorating. It's exciting, being on that knife edge. The craziness, anxiety, the tears and conflict. Who wouldn't want to be a part of that?

(**NICOLE** *just slowly and silently raises her hand)*

You'd be surprised. It's very entertaining. Better than any Play.

NICOLE. I can see why she likes you. I'm sure she'll miss you a great deal.

KATHERINE. Do you? I don't think she'll even remember my name, in a year or two. It's quite shocking how quickly they forget us.

(In the distance, we hear the audience begin to applaud)

(The sound of the applause grows in volume as the lights fade out on the dressing room and rise on the "stage" area.)

Scene Three

(**LYDIA** *is revealed in a deep bow to the audience (now us, so she faces downstage). She is lit in a wide but solo spotlight. The audience applause is now loud and tumultuous with cheers, shouts and yells of brava!* **LYDIA** *raises her head, her face beaming with satisfaction. She casts her eyes around the entire auditorium, opens her arms wide as though welcoming their embrace, and then bows deeply again.* **MARGARET** *enters her spotlight with a bouquet of flowers.* **LYDIA** *looks delighted and takes them. She now quietens the audience so that she can speak. When they are quiet, she considers her words for a moment*)

LYDIA. Ladies and gentlemen. Friends. This night -

(*She realises* **MARGARET** *is standing too close to her and gestures for her to move away*)

(**MARGARET** *takes a step back, but is still lit at the edge of the spotlight*)

(*To* **MARGARET**) …A little more… One more step.

(**MARGARET** *takes one more step back so that he is now out of the spotlight completely and in darkness.* **LYDIA** *looks pleased*)

…That's better.

(*She returns to face her audience*)

So… What is there to say? I have nothing written down, no speech. If only Chekhov were here to come up with a few lines! Well… (*she thinks*) Tonight, dear people, is both ending and beginning. And it makes me reflect on why I chose this profession. This profession that has consumed my entire life for so many decades. What brought me to it, at the beginning, wasn't the craft, not the words, the costumes. In truth, it just seemed at the time, the best way to manage my life. As a child, I could never walk into a room with confidence, and as a young woman, I could never be relaxed in the company of strangers. You have to know *why* you want to be an actress. And if your own skin doesn't seem to fit – then playing parts in a world of make believe is a fine way to find your place, to feel you belong. …A journalist once asked me what I loved most about doing this. And I talked of working with an ensemble, I talked of entertaining the public, of creativity and discovery. I talked of Chekhov and Shakespeare and Ibsen. …But it wasn't the truth. What I love – and I'm almost ashamed to admit it - is the applause. They'll tell you that's insecurity, the lack of love and approval you had as a child, the need for some sort of validation. But they've never stood here and actually heard it. Experienced the intense feeling when it washes over you. To some actors, it's nothing. The last moment of work before the run to the bus. But for me, it's everything. It's my drug. And I shall miss it. …Though tonight… somehow…I was no longer the young girl still trying to find her place. Nor the insecure woman waiting for her applause. Tonight I enjoyed the words of the drama, I found new meaning in them, new challenges in the eyes of the other actors, new ideas. I think tonight, knowing it was the end, it became purely about the craft. Almost for the first time. How unexpected. That on a night of such applause, that I was less of myself, and more of The Actress. …That is the parting gift you have given to me. And it was a genuine surprise, gratefully received. …Goodnight. …Goodbye. Thank you to each and every one of you that put me in the warmth of the spotlight. I shall miss you. And the warmth. And everything.

(Another bow. We hear the audience applaud enthusiastically. **LYDIA** *walks out of the spotlight and off of the stage. The spotlight fades to blackout)*

Scene Four

(Lights rises again on the dressing room. The roar of applause heard in the distance.)

KATHERINE. So that's it. The end of an era. ...I need to get everything ready.

(KATHERINE now checks that everything is ready for LYDIA's return and prepares some more herbal tea)

NICOLE. Have I got time for a cigarette?

KATHERINE. Go next door, the room's empty.

(NICOLE leaves. KATHERINE clears the cups away and then sprays the room with perfume. Shortly, LYDIA enters. She shuts the door behind herself and then clings to it. A deep breath)

KATHERINE. Your speech was lovely.

LYDIA. Chekhov would have written it better. Bloody playwrights. They're always *dead* just when you need them.

(LYDIA gives KATHERINE her bouquet and then moves from the door and into the centre of the room. She lowers her head so that KATHERINE can easily remove the wig and the hairnet. She then gives LYDIA a towel and she dries her own hair)

LYDIA. It was so hot out there. I thought I was going to melt.

KATHERINE. I'll get you some water.

(A knock on the door)

LYDIA. Already!? My god they're fast!

HARRIET. *(Beyond the door)* It's Harriet. ...Hello?

LYDIA. What did you do, Harriet? *Run* all the way here?

HARRIET. I couldn't wait another second to see you.

LYDIA. Well, hold your horses a moment longer, I'm still not out of my costume.

HARRIET. *(Still beyond the door)* Well, hurry then!

(**KATHERINE** *helps* **LYDIA** *out of her costume*)

…You were exquisite. …Delicious!

LYDIA. *(To* **KATHERINE***)* She makes me sound like a dessert.

HARRIET. I could eat you up!

LYDIA. There you are, what did I tell you?

KATHERINE. *(Chuckling)* What do you want to put on?

LYDIA. The dressing robe, the violet one.

HARRIET. Do you need another minute? Or can I come in now? …Lydia? I want to gobble you up. Yum, yum. Yum, yum!

LYDIA. *(To* **KATHERINE***)* Why is there never a large rifle around when you need one?

(**KATHERINE** *helps* **LYDIA** *put on the dressing robe and tie it up*)

…How am I?

KATHERINE. You look wonderful.

LYDIA. No, I look terrible. You're so clever when you don't tell the truth. Let her in.

(**KATHERINE** *opens the door and* **HARRIET** *bursts in, her arms spread wide*)

HARRIET. Oh, Lydia!

LYDIA. Oh sit down! Stop making a fuss.

(She gives her a huge embrace)

HARRIET. A night of nights! I could scream!

LYDIA. Oh, please don't bother.

(**NICOLE** *enters the room, cigarette in hand*)

Nicole! Oh, my angel!

(She goes to her daughter and takes the cigarette from her)

You have your mother's timing. Clever girl.

(She takes a deep drag on the cigarette and then puts it out)

NICOLE. So it went well?

LYDIA. Yes. *(She embraces her)* Yes. And you were here. Which is best of all.

*(*MARGARET *and* PAUL *now enter the room.* MARGARET *is carrying the vase from the play)*

PAUL. Ah – so this is where the party is. Lydia - you were a marvel. I couldn't have done it better myself.

HARRIET. We should have champagne. *(To* KATHERINE*)* Is there champagne?

KATHERINE. Yes, lots of it. Give me a hand, Nicole.

(As the conversation continues, NICOLE *and* KATHERINE *prepare two bottles of champagne and glasses.* LYDIA *sees the vase)*

LYDIA. And why have you brought that vase here? Is it full of vodka?

MARGARET. This is my souvenir. A gift from the producers. To thank me for all I've had to put up with.

LYDIA. In other words, you stole it when nobody was looking?

MARGARET. Either way – it's mine!

PAUL. I must say, Lydia, on stage tonight, you looked twenty years younger.

HARRIET. She did! That's true! It was magical.

PAUL. I thought the applause would never end.

HARRIET. And the speech –

PAUL. Yes. Very interesting, I thought.

HARRIET. *So* moving.

PAUL. Almost real. As though you hadn't been planning it for weeks.

LYDIA. I hadn't. Not at all.

PAUL. That's very unlike you. Perhaps you *are* changing.

MARGARET. Well, it's about time.

(At this point the champagne corks pop. A vocal reaction from everybody. They each grab a glass as **NICOLE** *and* **KATHERINE** *pour the drinks)*

HARRIET. Somebody should make a speech. ...Perhaps I -

*(***HARRIET*** *moves herself to the centre of the room, ready to propose a toast, but without having thought about what she wants to say)*

Gathered friends. On an occasion such as this. On such a grand and important - ...Oh, Lydia. Dear Lydia. When we... When I... Erm – wait, wait, let me just - ...I know – so – Lydia – we raise our glasses and - ...hang on, just a second –

LYDIA. Why don't we do this later once you've rehearsed?

HARRIET. Sorry. I need a good director.

LYDIA. *(At* **MARGARET***)* Well unfortunately there isn't one of those for *miles*!

PAUL. Oh, sod the speeches, let's just drink the damn stuff.

(There is vocal agreement from everybody and they all drink their champagne. At this moment, **CHARLES** *falls through the door, seriously out of breath)*

CHARLES. Chair! Quickly!

LYDIA. Charles! I thought we agreed –

CHARLES. Never mind that.

LYDIA. Oh you silly man.

(She takes her chair to **CHARLES***, who slumps onto it)*

You'll do yourself an injury.

CHARLES. Don't worry about me. I'm a picture of health. ...Anybody got any oxygen?

PAUL. Try the champagne – it has bubbles in it.

*(***PAUL*** *gets another glass of champagne from* **NICOLE***)*

CHARLES. Champagne, yes. *(To* **LYDIA***)* You were extraordinary tonight. I couldn't wait a minute longer to see you so that I could tell you. You took my breath away. Even more than the stairs.

LYDIA. Please – no more compliments. I can't take it. *(To everyone)* You're all very kind, but I don't want any more compliments tonight.

PAUL. Really? Are we in the right room?

HARRIET. *(Trying to get everybody's attention)* I'm sorry. I'm so sorry everyone. But I'm ready now. Let me start again.

(They all ignore **HARRIET**. **PAUL** *passes* **CHARLES** *his glass of champagne)*

PAUL. Here you are, old chap. Drink it slowly.

CHARLES. Thank you. Cheers everyone!

PAUL. So – you're Charles? "Geneva" Charles?

CHARLES. Yes. Have we met? *(To* **LYDIA**, *joking)* Not another of your ex-lovers is it?

*(***PAUL*** looks at* **LYDIA**, *laughing)*

LYDIA. *(Changing subject)* - Does everyone have another drink? Top them all up, Nicole.

*(***NICOLE*** and* **KATHERINE** *re-fill all the glasses)*

PAUL. Well, Lydia, you did say you wanted a rest. *(Looking at Charles)* And I think we can safely guarantee that.

LYDIA. Paul - shut up and sit on the sofa.

PAUL. Yes, Ma'am.

*(***PAUL*** goes and sits of the sofa, a big smile on his face.* **NICOLE** *is offering* **MARGARET** *more champagne)*

MARGARET. No, no more for me. I must go and visit the other cast members before they leave. Goodbye Lydia. I hope the Swiss air cleanses you. And now for *my* grand exit!

*(***MARGARET*** exits, extremely awkwardly, with her vase)*

CHARLES. She's a little odd. She's the one courting the director, isn't she? *(***LYDIA*** nods)* I've not met the director yet.

LYDIA. Neither have we! Apart from the odd murmur. He's an extremely strange man. But all directors are. A very odd bunch. Really - they should put them all on display in a museum. People would be fascinated.

HARRIET. *(Persevering)* I think I now know what I want to say.

LYDIA. The question is, Harriet, does anyone want to listen? *(She laughs)*

HARRIET. *(Disgruntled)* Well I think that's a bit –

LYDIA. *(A sudden thought, interrupting)* Chocolates! Are there chocolates?

NICOLE. I think Katherine ate them all.

KATHERINE. I did not! They're right here.

(**KATHERINE** *presents a box of chocolates to* **LYDIA**. *Meanwhile,* **HARRIET** *pours her champagne into the jar with the flower stalks and then re-fills her champagne glass to the brim with brandy)*

LYDIA. I shall miss people bringing me chocolates.

(She takes a chocolate)

CHARLES. We do have chocolate in Switzerland, you know.

LYDIA. Oh yes – of course you do!

CHARLES. I shall buy you some every morning. Get up while you're still asleep, and walk to the shops.

PAUL. I hope the shops aren't up a hill. You won't see him all day.

CHARLES. Sorry – what was that?

PAUL. Nothing, I was just - *(to* **LYDIA***)* I'd really like to hear about Switzerland. Tell me about it.

LYDIA. Oh for goodness sake - …You're not the slightest bit interested in –

PAUL. I am! Really I am. If you're going to leave all this for that place, then I want to know what's so special about it. - Is it beautiful?

LYDIA. Beyond beautiful. Across the lake you can see the Alps - iced in white, and their perfect reflection across the cool water. And birds fly overhead as the occasional boat drifts by, past the edge of the lake and the wooden jetties and charming small villages. And in the spring, there are small colorful flowers everywhere at the corner of your eye. And crisp air on a gentle wind.

CHARLES. That's right, exactly right.

LYDIA. And that's not all. There are so many places to visit – French, Italian, German. Each with their own restaurants. You can have croissants, pizza and sausages, each in their own language, all in one afternoon.

PAUL. Won't you get very fat?

LYDIA. Oh, I do hope so. The food is exceptional, the people polite, the streets clean. I used to dream of a place like that. And now it's mine. ...And what's more, I get to share it all with Charles.

PAUL. And what will you do all day – with Charles? Apart from eat?

LYDIA. *(To Charles)* Oh, the time rushes by when we're together, doesn't it?

CHARLES. We talk for hours. Wonderful conversations.

(He starts to cough on the word "conversations" but recovers quickly)

LYDIA. It's true. We never run out of dialogue. Though sometimes I go completely quiet and just listen intently. Like a student in love with her teacher. He's a fascinating, miraculous man. The love of my life.

PAUL. So you finally got everything you wanted?

LYDIA. I did.

PAUL. *(Not very convincingly)* Good. Good for you.

HARRIET. *(To herself, drinking her brandy, snidely)* Yes, good for you...

(MARGARET appears again, now without the vase)

MARGARET. They want the costumes for the truck.

(Nothing happens)

...The truck, the truck! Costumes!

(**KATHERINE** *now reacts, gathering the costumes up*)

MARGARET. Out with the old, in with the new!

KATHERINE. Could you take the wig, Margaret?

MARGARET. I could.

(**MARGARET** *picks up the wig mounted on its mannequin wig stand*)

I might see if I can take this home with me. Put it on display in the hall. - On the end of a spike!

(*She laughs.* **MARGARET** *exits,* **KATHERINE** *following her with her arms full of costumes*)

LYDIA. I'm beginning not to like her…

NICOLE. Perhaps you should start clearing everything else away? Doesn't it all have to be gone tonight?

LYDIA. I'm delaying it. I'm not ready for that – not yet.

NICOLE. Why not?

LYDIA. Oh, Nicole – the last show is always a very strange affair, even on the most insignificant of runs. Don't you see all that activity in the corridors? It's like a party, a great buzz of excitement, tears and smiles and the chaotic exchange of phone numbers. But then each actor will leave, with laughter still ringing in the air and a cheery wave. And then it stops. And as you watch each of them walk down the street, they look terribly lonely. That's the thing about it, you see. After all the company and chatter, after the applause and elation, they – we - walk home alone. It's why so many actors drink heavily. Delaying that walk as long as we can. And that's who actors are – the happiest, saddest people you'll ever meet.

(*She takes a drink*)

CHARLES. …But you're not sad tonight. You're walking home with me.

LYDIA. …Yes. And on the eve of a big adventure. …So – you're right - we might as well make a start. (*To* **NICOLE**) - Nicole, would you help me clear these cards?

(**NICOLE** *starts to clear the cards from around the mirror and around the room*)

…Anybody need another drink?

HARRIET. Ah yes – thank you.

(*She immediately helps herself, re-filling her champagne glass with more brandy*)

NICOLE. (*Referring to the cards*) Do you really know all these people?

LYDIA. Actors mostly. Each card carries a recollection of some old show or other. This profession leaves you with so many potent memories.

NICOLE. You're very lucky. To have found something that you love to do.

(*Examining one of the cards more closely*)

That gives you so much to look back on.

LYDIA. I *am* lucky. And I know it. You'll be lucky too.

NICOLE. (*A look at* **LYDIA**) Actually, I'm not sure I will. I've a feeling I'll never discover what I want to do with my life.

LYDIA. Nicole…

NICOLE. Oh, I'll fill it up one way or another. But I've still no idea where I'm going.

PAUL. Don't be silly.

NICOLE. Oh, it's not silly. Hardly anybody amongst my friends has any path, any target. We're the lost generation. Just drifting along.

(*She looks at all the cards now in her hand, then back at* **LYDIA**)

…But then I see you. And how you knew what you wanted to do from such a young age. I'm really jealous of that. You've never been lost, have you?

LYDIA. Finding your career doesn't always bring you happiness.

NICOLE. No. But you know who you are.

LYDIA. *(Touching her cheek, affectionately)* And we'll find who you are, Nicole. It just takes time. ...And I've plenty of that now. I can help you. You can come and stay with us for as long as you like.

NICOLE. I like it here.

LYDIA. Well, I won't *be* here, my darling. Silly. *(Changing subject)* ...Now, all these flowers must go down to the stage door. We could take an armful each. Not you, Charles, obviously. Harriet can take extra.

HARRIET. *(Aggressively)* No, Harriet can't!

LYDIA. *(To* HARRIET*)* What's the matter with you?

HARRIET. I had a speech!

*(*LYDIA *sees her glass and the emptying brandy bottle)*

LYDIA. Have you drunk all my brandy? Why didn't you drink the other brandy, the one you bought? Mine was expensive! Honestly – it's half gone – I thought you only took 10% of everything? *(An exasperated outlet of breath)* Anyway...*(to the others)* Come on, now, let's get rid of these bloody flowers. Paul – take the bunches closest to you, and Nicole – pick up a few of those big bouquets.

*(*PAUL *and* NICOLE *do as they're told,* LYDIA *organising everything)*

...And Harriet, you can take those ones in pots at the back.

HARRIET. Nobody can leave yet – we haven't made a toast!

LYDIA. We're not doing a toast, we're clearing the flowers away.

*(*PAUL *and* NICOLE *are now standing with arms full of flowers)*

CHARLES. Save me one for my buttonhole.

LYDIA. You could have a whole forest for your buttonhole. Why don't we take a few of the single roses and press them into our books?

PAUL. Books!? You *read* now?! When did that madness start?

HARRIET. I'd like to propose a toast, to Lydia and –

LYDIA. *(Ignoring* **HARRIET***)* I never used to read at all. Not books. Always scripts and more scripts. But books are so wonderful – you can get lost in them completely. Charles has given me a complete set of -

HARRIET. *(Interrupting, raising her voice)* Could I finally speak!?

LYDIA. Oh will you shut up, Harriet!

HARRIET. *(Losing his temper)* No – *you* shut up! Damn you to hell!!

(Everyone freezes)

(Loudly) It's not your spotlight any more. I have something to say! And I'd be grateful if you'd show some courtesy and bloody well listen to it!

LYDIA. Harriet! You're shouting! *(Shouting)* I will not have shouting in my dressing room!

HARRIET. It's not *your* dressing room any more, Lydia. Beatrice Lovechild starts Tuesday in "Cleopatra" - so she's in and you're out!

LYDIA. I don't appreciate your tone.

HARRIET. You don't appreciate anything. Or anybody! You never have. Making us all run around after you like bloody puppies. Your constant whining and complaining and nothing is ever right – or good enough – and all we ever do is give you the best of everything. The best theatres, the best parts, the best salary, and it's never enough. Never. There are actresses, thousands of them, that would weep with joy at the prospect of just one night standing in your shoes. And you spit on each and every one of them.

LYDIA. *(Astonished)* What gives you the right to -

HARRIET. Have you thought for one second about what happens when you walk out that door? …The people that will get trampled under your feet? I have nothing when you're gone. Nothing. Did you ever ask me if *I* wanted to retire? Did you? Well I don't! I *don't* want

to retire. I want a life – more of my life here. I want
people to continue to see me, for gentlemen to tip
their hats. To be respected. To be at the centre of it.
And you care nothing for that. You care nothing for
what will happen to me. And what *will* happen to me?
I'm finished. Already forgotten. You selfish, selfish,
heartless woman!

(**HARRIET** *now bursts into tears. She grabs the box of
tissues. Everyone is momentarily speechless*)

LYDIA. Well, I …

CHARLES. *(Standing, to* **HARRIET***)* I think you had better
leave.

HARRIET. That's right – throw me out on the street!

(She heads for the door, but turns back)

…Selfish. *(Screaming)* Selfish!

(**HARRIET** *leaves, slamming the door behind her*)

PAUL. *(After a short pause)* …Come on – be honest. Am I the
only one who enjoyed that?

LYDIA. I can hardly – …

NICOLE. Just forget about it. She'd been drinking all
evening.

LYDIA. It's not my fault her client list is an actor's graveyard.
Why is that my fault? Given her absolute incompetence
at selecting people, she should be grateful that she's
had *me* all these years. I didn't even want an agent!

CHARLES. Lydia, calm down.

LYDIA. I didn't. All they do is get in the way. What is their
point? What is their purpose?

PAUL. To keep you in control, I expect.

LYDIA. Nobody's asking you, Paul. You don't know a thing
about it. Oh God, I can't breathe in here. All these
bloody flowers – it's suffocating. It's my right to retire
whenever I want. To do what I want, go where I want,
when I want. Isn't it? …For God's sake, that's not a
rhetorical question – isn't it!?

(All contribute a general "yes")

Now get those flowers out of here before I catch hay fever.

*(**CHARLES** starts to cough. **PAUL** and **NICOLE** head for the door with the flowers, **PAUL** pausing to make a quick comment to **CHARLES** as he goes)*

PAUL. If you're not still with us by the time I get back – it was nice to meet you.

*(**PAUL** and **NICOLE** exit. **CHARLES** goes to follow them out)*

LYDIA. …Where are you going?

CHARLES. I'm not accustomed to all this shouting. I need some air. I'll wait for you by the exit.

LYDIA. So that's how it'll be, is it? Whenever anything unpleasant happens – you just run out of here as fast as you can?

CHARLES. I wish I *could* run out of here.

LYDIA. I need support sometimes. Somebody to lean on. Can I lean on you, Charles? Can I? Or will you just topple over?

CHARLES. We'll discuss this when you decide to be more civil.

LYDIA. Civil?

CHARLES. Civil, yes. Do you even know what that means?

LYDIA. Of course I do, you Swiss fool.

CHARLES. Fine – the fool is leaving.

LYDIA. Good. Just go, would you! Go!

CHARLES. We'll forget about this for the next 24 hours. And then we can discuss it all by the lake.

LYDIA. Yes, or throw ourselves in it!

*(**KATHERINE** returns)*

KATHERINE. What was all the noise?

LYDIA. The sound of my agent's career coming to an end. It was deafening.

KATHERINE. You're clearing the flowers? Shall I –

LYDIA. Yes, take a few bunches – and help Charles down the stairs. Or push him down them, whichever takes your fancy. I don't care either way at this moment.

(KATHERINE *gathers up some more of the flowers*)

CHARLES. I think the best thing we can do is get you as quickly as possible out of this building. Theatres are clearly not good for your state of mind. From what I've seen, you're all half crazy.

LYDIA. Only "half"?!

(KATHERINE *assists* CHARLES *out the door*)

CHARLES. (*To* KATHERINE) We have very few actors in Switzerland. That's why it's so quiet...!

(*They exit.* LYDIA *attempts to calm herself. She is now alone in the room. She shuts her eyes and draws a very deep breath. When she opens her eyes again, she suddenly realises how empty the room is. She wanders around the room, touching the wall, the furniture, her make up box. She is suddenly overcome and begins to cry. She puts her hands to her face to stop herself. Shortly,* PAUL *appears in the doorway, leaning against the frame*)

PAUL. ...Are you alright?

LYDIA. No. I don't think I am. It's suddenly so empty.

PAUL. To be fair – a little less empty now I'm standing here. ...Have you been crying?

LYDIA. No – just a drop or two. I'm surprised, I thought I'd emptied that supply during the show. I think *real* tears come from a different part of you. ...I'm a little frightened.

PAUL. You? You're not frightened of anything.

LYDIA. I didn't used to be. But I'm getting older.

PAUL. Don't be ridiculous. Actresses don't get older. They just get better wigs and more make-up.

(LYDIA *laughs a little*)

LYDIA. That's true. Until the moment arrives when you can no longer learn your lines. Then you age so fast, it knocks you off your feet. ...Are you just going to stand there? You look like you're holding the wall up.

PAUL. That might be necessary. Word has it that when you leave this building, the roof will cave in. The building will die without you.

LYDIA. I'd love that to be true. But the next wagon of young performers is already rolling into town.

PAUL. ...Do you need a hug? I'm fully available for hugs. Or – for that matter - something a bit more -

LYDIA. Don't make me slap you again. It's very hard on the palms.

PAUL. Then I'll stay right here, if you don't mind. My dentist will appreciate it. I'll just look at you from a distance.

LYDIA. There's no law against that.

PAUL. There should be – you don't know what I'm thinking... *(A moment)* ...Why did you ever leave me?

LYDIA. Oh Paul – not now.

PAUL. Well, it makes no sense.

(**PAUL** *takes a quick look at himself in the mirror)*

...I'm gorgeous.

LYDIA. No, you're arrogant and short sighted. It's not quite the same thing.

PAUL. I think if you and I had just given it more of a chance -

LYDIA. More of a chance!? Paul - you had a dozen affairs!

PAUL. A dozen! My god you exaggerate. - It was no more than ten.

LYDIA. Ha!

PAUL. *And* you'd already left me by that point.

LYDIA. We were still married.

PAUL. Only technically. The house was on sale, you'd removed your possessions *and* you'd told me you never wanted to see me again.

LYDIA. Which didn't work. You followed me around the entire country during the tour of "Hamlet" – I couldn't get rid of you.

PAUL. I wanted to patch things up.

LYDIA. And how did you go about that? By having sex with the actress playing Ophelia! I was so humiliated. The poor girl didn't know what hit her.

PAUL. I wouldn't put it quite like that.

LYDIA. And you had liaisons with other females in the play. Including the blonde who played the Lady's Maid. Or if the rumours were true, *both* the Lady's Maids. By the end of the run, you'd slept with every woman in Denmark!

PAUL. With you rejecting me on a nightly basis, what was I supposed to do? I loved you! Before "Hamlet" I never even looked at another woman.

(A look from **LYDIA***)* - I didn't! I was there for you.

LYDIA. If you were, I didn't see you.

PAUL. Then maybe you should have looked up from your *scripts* occasionally? It's not easy competing for your attention with a thousand cheering people. *Being* in the theatre is all very well, but when it's all you talk about and all you think about, what room is there left for any kind of genuine human relationship? Damn it, Lydia. If you can walk away from it with that old banker, then why couldn't you walk away from it for me?

LYDIA. I don't know.

PAUL. That's not an answer.

LYDIA. It's all I have. I can't explain how I felt about something over a decade ago. I hardly remember what I was feeling yesterday. It just didn't work. That's my pathetic answer. I'm sorry. But I do – for what it's worth – regret it …sometimes. …And just for the record, I'm pretty sure Ophelia regrets it too!

PAUL. I find that very hard to believe. …Whatever happened to her, by the way?

LYDIA. Well, she didn't run off to a nunnery, if that's what you were hoping. You're not *that* good. I think she ended up in *Charley's Aunt.* …But we don't have to talk about her, do we?

PAUL. No, let's talk about you. …And me.

LYDIA. You're exhausting.

PAUL. *(A smile)* So they tell me.

(**LYDIA** *sits down, and takes a deep breath. She then glances around the room)*

LYDIA. …Isn't this room terrible? They're the most awful places once they start to clear everything away. All of a sudden you're at a funeral.

PAUL. Let's go for a walk.

LYDIA. A walk? …Yes, alright. I'd quite like to have a final wander around the stage. …You'll like being there once the show's over. It has a very special atmosphere. Haunted, but friendly.

(**KATHERINE** *comes back in)*

Katherine - are there still lights on the stage?

KATHERINE. There's a ghost light, that's all.

LYDIA. Perfect – for old ghosts like us.

(**LYDIA** *picks up the box of chocolates)*

KATHERINE. Charles is waiting for you downstairs.

LYDIA. I know. We're just going to have a last few minutes before… *(referring to the items left on her dressing table)* - Would you clear those final things? Pop them all into my make-up case?

KATHERINE. Of course. I'll leave it with Charles.

LYDIA. Thank you. You're an angel.

(**LYDIA** *kisses* **KATHERINE**)

…I'll miss you.

KATHERINE. Will you?

(**LYDIA** *does not respond, just a little smile. She leaves with* **PAUL**. **KATHERINE** *quickly clears the final items on the table and puts them all into the make-up box. Everything except the powder puff compact. She thinks for a moment, and then puts the compact into her pocket. Lights fade down on the dressing room*)

End of Scene Four

Scene Five

(The "stage" area. A single ghost light, on a stand is the only strong light on stage. But blue and red working lights upstage pick out other details)

(LYDIA and PAUL walk onto the stage and into the area lit by the ghost light. LYDIA sits on the chair and PAUL perches himself on another piece of furniture, or sits on the floor of the stage)

LYDIA. …Chocolate?

(She offers him her box of chocolates and he takes one and chucks it in his mouth)

PAUL. These are good. Who bought you these?

LYDIA. I don't recall. One of my admirers.

PAUL. Which one?

(LYDIA looks at the label on the box of chocolates. Somewhat horrified by who sent them, she throws the box across the stage)

PAUL. Don't you like anybody you've been to bed with?

LYDIA. I did when I went to bed with them. But at some point they feel they have to tell me all about themselves. And it's generally downhill from there.

PAUL. You always had terrible taste in boyfriends. …But good taste in husbands.

LYDIA. Well, you would say that.

PAUL. And I just did say that.

(PAUL gets up and gives her a quick kiss)

LYDIA. Don't. That's not why we're here.

PAUL. I thought perhaps you might - Well, you know… We did rather enjoy our little tumble in the bushes – didn't we?

LYDIA. That was a display of silliness that will not happen again. It was before the show. I was very nervous, scared, - ...I don't know what I was – but I wasn't myself.

PAUL. Oh, it was *you* alright. I saw you in there. And it wasn't a bad way to say hello. Or goodbye. ...Can I just ask – this Charles. How old is he exactly?

LYDIA. Does it matter? Age is only a number. There's no law says you have to act your age. It's no more sensible than acting the number of your house. And Charles – whatever his number is – has the mind of a vigorous 40 year old and the sexual libido of a teenage boy.

PAUL. A teenage boy? You mean no idea what he's doing, but lots of enthusiasm?

LYDIA. He is a wonderful man. You'll never spend enough time with him to realise that. But it's something I know for sure.

PAUL. Nothing's for sure these days. ...Lydia, are you really going?

LYDIA. Oh Paul, you're so ridiculous. Can't you ever accept things as they are?

PAUL. I just thought – when you were on the stage – the speech at the end of the show. I thought I saw something. A flicker of doubt.

LYDIA. You were mistaken. And I shall prove it to you. In a year's time, you can come and visit us. And see how settled we are, how happy we are.

PAUL. How *cold* you are.

LYDIA. You don't notice the cold because it's so charming there. So different. So *clean.*

PAUL. You see, I'm always worried when the foremost adjective used to describe somewhere is "clean". Who wants to live somewhere because it's "clean"? I would have thought that's the last thing you should care about. If there aren't a few bottles in the street, a rat or two and a bit of blood and urine, how exciting can a place be? I don't want to live somewhere sanitary, I want to be somewhere sexy, a little bit dangerous. At

least then you know you're alive. …You can change
your mind.

LYDIA. No.

PAUL. You can! And you should. If you're not absolutely
sure where you're going – then stay where you are. …
Okay, so I saw that on a poster. But it doesn't mean it's
not true.

LYDIA. I need a script. That's my problem. To tell me what
to do. But I am certain that I've had enough of this
absurd theatrical life.

PAUL. But without it – who are you?

LYDIA. So if you know me so well - tell me how it ends.

PAUL. It's for you to decide, Lydia.

LYDIA. But I don't know. I don't know how it ends.

(NICOLE enters at this moment)

NICOLE. …I do.

*(She crosses to them. NICOLE and PAUL sit on the floor
on either side of LYDIA. Then LYDIA gets off of her chair
and sits on the floor between them. They all hold hands
and lean on each other. Shortly, CHARLES walks on to
the edge of the stage)*

CHARLES. I'm waiting for you. Are you coming? Lydia? Are
you coming?

(There is a long pause)

LYDIA. …Yes, Charles.

*(LYDIA lets go of their hands. She gets up and crosses
the stage towards CHARLES. He holds his arms out to
welcome her, smiling. Before she reaches CHARLES, PAUL
says something)*

PAUL. Lydia –

(LYDIA pauses, standing still)

…You'll be back. You have to come back.

(She turns back to look at PAUL and NICOLE)

LYDIA. …Maybe…one day…

(She looks towards the auditorium. Then back at **PAUL***)*

…Do you think the audience will wait for me?

PAUL. I have no idea. …But *I* will.

*(***LYDIA*** smiles at him. The actors now freeze in position.)*

(The lighting changes - the ghost light fading out and the scattered lights upstage rising to mark the actors in a soft silhouette. We hear, in the distance, a piece of music that **LYDIA** *had played earlier in her dressing room.)*

(When this has all been firmly established – the curtain slowly closes, or the lights slow fade to blackout.)

The End